Veronese

Cover
Juno Pouring Her Gifts Upon Venice, *detail, 1553-1554.*
Venice, Doge's Palace, Sala del Consiglio dei Dieci.

Texts by Stefano Zuffi
Translation by Richard Sadleir

Photograph Credits
Alinari/Lauros Archive - Giraudon, Florence
Camera Photo, Venice
Electa Archive, Milan
Fototecnica, Vicenza
Paolo Manusardi, Milan
Photo Service Fabbri, Milan
Enrico Polidori, Genoa

BT

This volume was printed by Elemond S.p.a.
at the plant in Martellago (Venice) in 1996

Veronese

Electa/Art Books International

Paolo Caliari, called Il Veronese

"**W**e painters take the same licence that poets and madmen take." With these words Paolo Veronese defended his freedom as an artist before the Court of the Holy Inquisition in 1573. The judges had asked him to explain the presence of numerous elements in one of his spectacular paintings—the *Feast in the House of Levi*. The painter replied with a mixture of serene, open frankness and subtle, captious originality.

Veronese's splendid art develops between these two poles, which are only seemingly irreconcilable. On the one hand they are luminous and spontaneous, full of the pleasure of contemplating men and women with perfect bodies and clad in precious garments, smiling faces framed with jewels, gleaming buildings made of choice materials; and on the other, they record his concern to study in depth the latest developments in art, to grasp the secrets of Mannerist design and of Titianesque colour. In these ways Veronese worked out his own utterly personal and unmistakable style, which was totally different from that of his Venetian contemporaries.

Through the noble handling of scenic elements, a certain restrained theatricality, complete mastery of colour and a limpid purity in the architectural settings, Veronese sought to achieve an innate classicism, vivid and pleasing, with a naturally elegant harmony. His drawings played an important part in his work, though this has only recently been realized and adequately studied. And like another artist from mainland Italy, Palladio (born in Vicenza), Paolo Veronese constructed a new world of uncontaminated interior and exterior spaces, ready for the reception of a festive throng. The collaboration between the architect and the artist in the Villa Barbaro at Maser pro-

Presumed self-portrait as a hunter. Maser, Villa Barbaro.

duced one of the supreme creations of the Renaissance: the villa and its decoration are clearly made for each other, the fruit of a cultural project pursued with outstanding insight and intellectual planning, enriched by a knowledge of antiquity and the example of Central Italian classicism. Yet, at the same time, everything seems to spring naturally from the landscape itself. The harmonious proportions, the restrained splendour of the colour scheme and the interplay of spaces create a whole of inimitable beauty.

Veronese lived and worked in Venice at a time when the Serenissima increasingly needed images to sustain the "myth" of itself, when it was threatened by religious conflicts and wars with the Turks. He certainly enjoyed a more than satisfactory success, being summoned repeatedly to work in the Doge's Palace and other official buildings of the Republic; and the trial before the Inquisition had no effect on his career. Yet he remained essentially an isolated figure, widely admired but not imitated, his fame being bound up with the dream of a universe of joy that the political and religious events of the late 16th century conspired to doom.

Early Years: Between the Tradition of Verona and Mannerism (1528–1555)

Records show that Veronese was born in 1528, the last of five children of Gabriele, a stone-carver. His birthplace was Verona, in the heart of a strong and independent artistic tradition which left its mark on his work as a painter.

Since the time of the Della Scala reign, Verona had been a vigorous and independent artistic centre which at the same time allowed itself to be influenced by other currents, its geographical position making it a kind of link between the Veneto and eastern Lombardy. In the 16th century Verona had produced interesting painters (the Caroto family, Paolo Morando, Domenico Brusacorci and others), with many features in common: the animation of their figures, vivid expressiveness, an interest in mythological subjects, a talent for decorating and frescoing palaces and villas (with the climate favouring their preservation, unlike that of Venice).

Antonio Badile, Paolo's master, was a typical representative of this school. Under his teaching some of the most fertile and attractive decorative artists of the Renaissance grew up: Giambattista Zelotti, for instance, was a fellow pupil of Veronese and became a successful fresco painter who worked in numerous villas.

Paolo Caliari (whose surname "Veronese" appears only in the 1550s) completed his training in a stimulating environment, and at an important moment in the history of Venetian art. The 1540s saw the start of an intense rivalry with Central Italian art, and Mannerism in particular. The arrival of important Tuscan-Roman intellectuals and artists in Venice led to direct comparison between Titian's typically chromatic and naturalistic style and the Mannerist concept of drawing as the essential basis for an elegant, refined, and intellectualized art. The tradition of Venetian colourism was opposed to the teaching of the great masters at work in Florence and Rome, above all Michelangelo, then engaged on the painting of the *Last Judgement* in the Sistine Chapel.

The echoes of this debate reached the provinces and its effects appear clearly in the works produced by Veronese in his early twenties. Having just left Badile's workshop, he displayed the qualities that appear all through his work. The *Bevilacqua-Lazise Altarpiece* (Plate 1), now in the Museum of Castelvecchio in Verona, dates from 1548, and is his first important work. The composition is simple, with the figures arranged regularly on different planes, and reveals that the artist was still feeling his way. But the clarity of the architectural elements, the luminous colours combined with complicated, twisted poses and the nobility and elegance of the whole foreshadow the later style. With this work Veronese made his name as an original artist in his native Verona, and it was followed by a number of portraits.

In 1551 the architect Matteo Sanmicheli commissioned Veronese and Giambattista Zelotti to provide fresco decorations for the Villa Soranza at Treville, near Castelfranco Veneto. The villa was destroyed in 1818: the surviving fragments of fresco (most of which are in the sacristy of the cathedral of Castelfranco) together with earlier descriptions suggest that Paolo devised a complex scheme of ornamentation, with balustrades and *trompe l'œil* architecture framing mythical, historical and allegorical figures, often boldly foreshortened and projected towards the ceilings.

These skilfully intricate figures spread Veronese's fame beyond the confines of Verona, and in 1552 Cardinal Ercole Gonzaga commissioned an altarpiece for one of the four new altars designed by Giulio Romano for Mantua cathedral. This painting (the *Temptation of Saint Anthony*), is in the Caen Museum in Normandy (Plate 5). It is a highly articulated composition, with affinities with Titian's Mannerist paintings, but it also contains numerous innovations, such as the bright figure of the temptress in the background.

In 1553 Giovan Battista Ponchino, a modest Mannerist painter from Rome who admired and imitated Michelangelo, received a commission from the Consiglio dei Dieci to decorate the ceilings of three chambers in the Doge's Palace in Venice with allegorical canvases. He was allowed to choose his assistants, and the choice fell on Zelotti and Veronese. This was his entrance into the world of Venetian art. His share of the work was executed in 1553 and 1554, and completely eclipsed that of his fellow painters, with the result that he became "Il Veronese," to the exclusion of all others from the same city, and a Venetian by adoption. The celebrated painting of *Juno Pouring Her Gifts Upon Venice* (Plate 6), in the Sala del Consiglio dei Dieci, presents figures in complex, convoluted poses within a setting clearly designed according to the precepts of Mannerism, with an easy naturalness largely conferred by the limpid clarity of the use of light. Veronese's colouring was always fluid and variegated, quite unlike Titian's increasingly thick, heavy handling of pigment. This may have been the reason why Titian always looked favourably on Veronese, instead of seeing him as a rival, as happened with Tintoretto. Veronese, for his part, was clearly aware of Titian's work, and showed great interest in his methods of composition, though the final result may often seem quite different. A good example is the *Giustiniani Altarpiece* in San Francesco della Vigna (Plate 7), evidence of the rapid spread of his fame among the Venetian aristocracy. The composition repeats the scheme of the *Pesaro Altarpiece* painted thirty years earlier by Titian for the Basilica dei Frari.

Triumph of a Universe of Happiness (1555–1573)

In 1555 Veronese made Venice his permanent home, and in the same year he began work on a project that was to occupy many years to come: the decoration of the church of San Sebastiano, in the area of Le Zattere. His paintings here included altarpieces, large canvases in the presbytery, frescoes and organ cases. Among the earliest paintings are the three *Stories*

Saint Mark the Evangelist, pen and ink over a black pencil sketch, 286 × 191 cm. Dresden, G. Brühl Collection.

of Esther (Plate 8) on the ceiling. The preservation of all these works in their original place provides the best opportunity to study Veronese's striking command of perspective and brilliant colouring.

The church of San Sebastiano is not particularly well-known; but Veronese's work made it famous in his own day. Immediately after the completion of the *Stories of Esther*, the artist was called on to decorate the ceiling of the Libreria Marciana. This was the outcome of a kind of competition, the judge being Titian, the "patriarch" of Venetian painting. Veronese and six other young artists were involved, all to some extent members of the Mannerist school. Veronese painted three great roundels set in a rich wooden frame, with the allegories of *Honour*, *Arithmetic* and *Music* (Plate 10). This last painting above all reveals the confidence already achieved by Veronese, not yet thirty years old, in increasingly complex and sumptuous compositions with brilliantly vivid colours. Titian may have seen reminiscences of his own youthful work in these paintings, and awarded Veronese the first prize, a gold medal, so conferring official sanction on his success.

In the years around 1560 Veronese was busy with paintings for patrician families and Venetian institutions: he produced frescoes, portraits, and paintings for private devotion (such as the enchanting fair-haired *Madonnas* now in the Pinacoteca di Vicenza and the Uffizi) or for churches (an example is the painting for the high altar of San Sebastiano). But his interest led him increasingly toward scenes of huge size packed with figures. He favoured subjects—religious or profane—which allowed him to display dozens of figures in action and robed in a mixture of ancient and contemporary costumes. Even when these cheerful throngs were not justified by the literary sources, Veronese had no hesitation in introducing them freely. The crowdedness of the *Feast in the House of Simon* (Galleria Sabauda, Turin) is wholly justified; but the *Supper at Emmaus* in the Louvre (Plate 11) has about fifteen figures in modern dress in a variety of poses, a scheme that is certainly surprising and differs widely from the tradition.

The work that closed Veronese's youthful period and at the same time established the nature of his wonderful artistic maturity were the frescoes in the Villa Barbaro at Maser in the province of Treviso (Plates 12–15). The date when Marcantonio and Daniele Barbaro commissioned Palladio and Veronese to build and decorate their splendid villa on the lower slopes of the hills is uncertain. Palladio designed a villa of classical clarity yet absolutely original. The main block stands between two porticoed wings of outbuildings, while the rear faces onto a charming semicircular nymphaeum with a fountain in the middle. The interior is laid out in an unusual scheme; there is a cross-shaped chamber with four rooms at its sides and a larger salon facing the nymphaeum. Inside this highly articulated structure, Veronese created a second structure of *trompe l'œil* architecture, with the help of his brother Benedetto Caliari as "quadraturist," and with stucco work by the great sculptor Alessandro Vittoria. The impression this creates when one enters Villa Barbaro is of suddenly finding oneself in an ideal world populated by happy figures. The scheme of decoration was probably laid down by the learned Daniele Barbaro. It envisaged a series of symbolical images, most of which celebrate moral virtues and exalt the pagan divinities of agriculture. But in the hands of Veronese, this outline became the occasion for creating a host of smiling gods and goddesses, while the allegorical sig-

Allegory of Peace, black pencil, pen and ink, retouched with white lead on grey-blue paper, 272 × 202 cm. Haarlem, Teylers Museum.

nificances fell into the background. Certain details, like the little girl looking curiously out of a doorway or a shaggy lapdog wagging its tail next to a balustrade, create the illusion of actual contact between our physical world and the splendid and rarefied world of the frescoes.

The same exuberant splendour is irradiated by the immense, spectacular canvas of the *Marriage at Cana* (1562–1563), painted for the refectory of San Giorgio Maggiore and now in the Louvre where it has recently been restored (Plate 16). Within a great, symmetrical architectural frame of perfect classic form, there moves an immense crowd of figures (about 120 in all). Studded among them are the portraits of many of the leading personages of the day. Though the figure of Christ is clearly evident in the centre of the composition, the religious theme is clearly secondary to the general impression of a great contemporary festivity created by the painting.

By about 1565 Veronese seems to have become almost hectically busy. Naturally he employed trusted assistants, mostly members of the Caliari family, like his brother Benedetto and his son Carletto. Having completed the two large canvases for the presbytery of San Sebastiano, he used a simple approach in the *Family of Darius before Alexander*, now in the National Gallery, London (Plate 17), one of his favourite historical subjects because of the opportunity it gave to insert magnificent figures. For similar reasons this was one of the commonest themes of the 18th century. Verona also became a fertile field of work once more, with the *Marogna Altarpiece* in the church of San Paolo and the *Martyrdom of Saint George* in San Giorgio in Braida (1566).

But Veronese did not always indulge his exuberant vein. Though by the 1570s splendid canvases emerged regularly from his workshop (like the cycle of paintings made for the Cuccina family, in the Dresden Gemäldegalerie), there were also more restrained and delicately intimate works, and others that reveal a troubled sense of contemporary history, which were no less splendid than the mythical subjects he so often dealt with. The *Dream of Saint Helen* is a masterpiece of penetrating psychology and exquisite chromatic balance (now in the National Gallery, London; Plate 19). The echo of dramatic historical events appears in the *Allegory of the Battle of Lepanto* (Gallerie dell'Accademia in Venice), painted to celebrate the battle of 1571 that seemed to have granted a respite from the constant threat of the Turks. The *Crucifixion* in the Galleria di Palazzo Bianco, in Genoa, has iridescent gleams amid a dark, even murky, setting.

In 1572 Veronese added new variations on his favourite subject of festivities: the *Feast of Saint Gregory* in the Sanctuary of Monte Berico at Vicenza (Plate 21). This is one of the most successful examples of the genre, with the elegance of its architectural setting and the fluidity of its narration, rich yet essential. Also at Vicenza, in the church of Santa Corona, Veronese painted an *Adoration of the Magi* of great poetic force, with the light of the sky fading towards night yet still gleaming kindling brilliant colours in the splendid mantles of the Magi to create a festive atmosphere that is also mysteriously charged with intense mysticism.

The Decline of Venice's Glory and of Its Last Painter (1573–1588)

In 1573 Veronese was called on to replace a painting by Titian that perished in a destructive fire in the refectory of the Dominicans in SS. Giovanni e Paolo. He painted a great *Last Supper*, an explosive, spectacular work, with three great arches suggesting the proscenium of the classical stage, within which move dozens of brilliantly clad figures. These were difficult years: the problem of Lepanto, despite the brilliant naval victory, was still unsolved, the city's economy was failing, and following the Council of Trent religious disputes were daily growing fiercer. In consequence, the Tribunal of the Inquisition made objections to Veronese's great painting and summoned the artist for questioning. Their aim was to discover if Veronese had inserted such a large number of accessory figures to belittle the mystic significance of the episode. Certain details (such as a soldier with a bleeding nose, dwarfs jumping and jesters) were considered highly offensive. The minutes of the trial reveal Veronese's apparent candour; he replied briefly and calmly to all the questions, insisting that painters may be permitted certain "licences" in their handling of a subject.

The trial ended with a compromise: the painting was left intact in its place, Veronese left the figures as they were but changed the title to the *Feast in the House of Levi*, now in the Gallerie dell'Accademia in Venice (Plates 22–24).

This episode did not harm Veronese's career, and may even have added to his popularity. But it reveals a changed cultural climate, one that could be troubled by the joyous festivity of Veronese's paintings. The terrible plague of 1576, which killed Titian, added to the gloom over Venice's future. Veronese played a splendid yet ambiguous part: he was the last artist called on to celebrate the myth of the Serene Republic, yet he was also a witness to its decline.

Two magnificent paintings of 1575 restored Veronese to the height of celebrity: the *Martyrdom of Saint Justina*, on the high altar of the basilica of Santa Giustina in Padua (where he had taken up resi-

Presumed self-portrait. Malibu, The J. Paul Getty Museum.

Antonio Zona, *The First Meeting between the Young Paolo Veronese and Titian*. Venice, Accademia di Belle Arti.
The canvas, inspired by the Ottocento taste for melodrama, is a demonstration of Veronese's popularity in the 19th century.

dence temporarily), and the *Mystic Marriage of Saint Catherine* in the Gallerie dell'Accademia in Venice (Plate 27). Perhaps due to the merits of these two paintings, Veronese received a commission to decorate the Sala del Collegio in the Doge's Palace. Around the main subject (*Venice Welcomes Justice and Peace*, Plate 25) he arranged a series of paintings with complex shapes, in which he set some of his most charming inventions; here, as always, he was able to transform a symbolic image into a vivid living figure.

After Titian's death the Venetian Senate saw Veronese as the artist best able to continue the splendour of Venetian art, and he was repeatedly called on to work in the Doge's Palace. He repaid their confidence with a series of outstanding works, including the *Rape of Europa* (Plate 30) for the Sala dell'Anticollegio (1580). Further versions of the same subject emerged from Veronese's workshop; the same also happened with the delightful painting of the *Finding of Moses*, of which the finest version is probably that in the Prado.

In about 1580 Veronese began to concentrate on canvases of more moderate size, some of them quite small, often dealing with mythical subjects. These include some delightful idylls, such as *Mars and Venus Bound by Cupid* in New York's Metropolitan Museum (Plate 29), and *Venus and Adonis* in the Prado (Plate 31). These enchanting paintings seem to contain a vein of melancholy, leading to comparisons with the poetry of Tasso.

The celebrated shimmering colour of so many of his masterpieces was now slightly veiled; this appears clearly in the *Susanna and the Elders* in the Kunsthistorisches Museum in Vienna, the *Saint Antony Preaching to the Fishes* in the Galleria Borghese in Rome, and above all in the moving *Agony in the Garden* in the Brera Gallery, Milan (Plate 32), one of the most intense works from his last period.

In 1583 Veronese (then fifty-five) tackled his last large-scale painting, a huge oval of the *Triumph of Venice* for the Sala del Maggior Consiglio in the Doge's Palace (Plate 34). The handling of perspective is once again attractive, the brilliance of the colour overwhelming, yet the execution reveals in certain places the hand of assistants, and as a whole this last tribute to Venice strikes one as rather overwrought and less spontaneous than the canvases painted thirty years earlier in the same building.

Veronese's last years were troubled by health problems and embittered by deaths in his family. The slight tinge of melancholy that had appeared in his work turned to sadness and meditation. The last works of this painter, who had created a new Olympus on earth, are weighed down by a profoundly devotional spirit: the moving *Dead Christ* in St. Petersburg (Plate 35) and the dramatic *Miracle of Saint Pantaleon*, in the church of San Pantaleone in Venice (1587).

On 19 April 1588, at sixty years of age, Veronese died and was buried in his beloved church of San Sebastiano, where his tombstone can still be seen.

The Legacy

In the case of Veronese it is particularly appropriate to speak of his "legacy," since his assistants continued his firm in business under the name of "Eredi di Paolo" (Heirs of Paolo). These men were mediocre painters, who timidly approached the problem of recreating the aristocratic world and brilliant colouring of Veronese. Moreover, these artists were faced with a profoundly changed historical situation and different tastes. After their effort petered out, Venetian painting abandoned Veronese's approach for over a century. On the other hand, scholars continued to celebrate Veronese's work. Even more than in the 16th century, his colouring was praised by art writers in the 17th century, including Boschini and Ridolfi. True, his art tended to be seen exclusively in terms of brilliant richness of colour, which might seem reductive, but it meant that he was carefully studied by the masters of the 17th century, such as the Neapolitan painters Mattia Preti and Luca Giordano. Through their mediation Veronese's luminous freshness was revived by the Venetian artists, though they continued to favour a confused imitation of Tintoretto.

In this way Veronese became a model for 18th-century art. Sebastiano Ricci was the first to abandon the "gloomy" style of 17th century Venetian painting and seek inspiration directly from Veronese's vast, bright sunny compositions. Ricci even imitated the costumes and classical architectures of his paintings, clearing a path for the genius of Giovan Battista Tiepolo, the greatest interpreter of international Rococo. Tiepolo also made explicit reference to Veronese, and the European fortune of his painting led to a critical rediscovery of the painter from Verona.

The 18th-century critics, while commenting on a supposed weakness in Veronese's paintings of nudes, were fascinated by the richness of composition, complexity and clarity of his works. Neoclassical critics reproved him for a certain superficiality on the handling of historical subjects, but praised his technique. He was also fortunate in that his paintings were usually better preserved than his contemporaries', and this encouraged collectors, many of whose purchases have ended up in museums (Dresden, Vienna).

The favour his paintings enjoyed in the 18th and 19th centuries meant that unfortunately numerous works were moved from their original settings into museums. The galleries created in the Napoleonic period (the Gallerie dell'Accademia in Venice, the Brera in Milan, the Louvre) absorbed numerous canvases, some of great size which proved difficult to collocate (a problem still largely unresolved).

Following the late 19th and early 20th century critical studies, Italian critics began to explore Veronese in his complexity between the two wars (see Arslan, Fiocco, and Pallucchini). The affinities with Mannerism were examined, not without polemics, while restoration and new discoveries filled out the catalogue of his works considerably. He was restored to his context in Venetian culture, especially his contacts with the complex intellectual figure of Daniele Barbaro (the patron who commissioned the decorations for the Villa Maser).

In more recent years greater attention has been paid to Veronese's drawings, which cover a wide range of subjects and are highly interesting but had previously been neglected. As often happens, the fourth centenary of his death in 1988 provided a valuable opportunity to widen our knowledge of the artist: two exhibitions (in Venice and Verona) and numerous specialized studies brought much new information to light.

Where to See Veronese

Paolo Veronese's artistic career developed over a period of forty years (1548–1588), mostly spent in Venice. In this span the painter produced decorative cycles and works of great size, yet he never lost sight of the private market and also did portraits and other paintings in smaller formats. Veronese's catalogue numbers over three hundred works with sacred, mythological and allegorical subjects: the great majority are on canvas, except for some on ceiling panels and a number of celebrated frescoes.

The record of Veronese's output is substantially complete, though there are a few large gaps. The destruction of his works began in his own lifetime and continued until the fire in the Berlin Museum at the end of the last war, when four paintings from the Fondaco dei Tedeschi were destroyed, together with a vast mythological canvas painted for the Ca' Pisani in Venice.

The first serious loss was in the fire that ravaged the Doge's Palace on 20 December 1577. No fewer than five masterpieces with historical and allegorical themes were destroyed; the artist was then commissioned to replace them with an even richer decorative cycle.

The list of lost frescoes is particularly long. It opens with a youthful work, the decoration of the Villa Soranzo at Treville. The house was demolished in the early 19th century and only a few fragments were detached and preserved. No trace remains of the frescoes on the façade of the Palazzo Bellavite in Venice; those in Palazzo Trevisan in Murano are almost indecipherable. Even the Villa Barbaro cycle lacks the fresco on the central crossing, which simulated a pergola against the open sky. Now the surface is whitewashed.

Finally the huge canvas of *San Sebastian Before Diocletian*, formerly in the church of San Sebastiano in Venice, was marred by damp and destroyed in the 19th century.

Works in Italy

The specific interest of Veronese lies in the fact that many works are still in the settings for which they were painted and where they were executed, with a close bond between painting and architecture. Three examples are illuminating; the frescoes in the Villa Barbaro at Maser, the decorations for the church of San Sebastiano and those in the six chambers of the Doge's Palace in Venice. About one third of Veronese's production has remained in Italy.

Venice

Apart from the early work, done when the painter was in his twenties, nearly all of Veronese's career took place in Venice. The city contains over half of the works still in Italy, and it is possible to trace an itinerary to include both celebrated works and less well-known ones in little frequented buildings.

The tour could well start with the church of San Pietro di Castello, which contains a late altarpiece with *Saints Peter, Paul and John*. Continuing beyond the Arsenal one comes to the church of San Francesco della Vigna, with two paintings marking the extremes of Veronese's career in Venice: the splendid *Giustiniani Altarpiece*, begun in 1551, and the late *Resurrection of Christ*. Not far from this is the basilica of Santi Giovanni e Paolo: the Capella del Rosario contains a significant part of the decorations originally painted for the church of San Nicolò dei Frari, now demolished.

On the way to Piazza San Marco one comes to the church of San Giuliano, which houses the very fine altarpiece of *Three Saints Before the Dying Christ*; a short deviation takes in San Luca, with the *Apparition of the Madonna to Saint Luke* on the high altar.

The Doge's Palace offers a vast and spectacular array of paintings by Veronese. Beginning with the early allegories of the *Triumph of Venice* in the Sala del Maggior Consiglio, the chambers of the seat of government of the Serenissima present an anthology of the main phases of the painter's career.

The three *tondi* of the splendid ceiling and the *Philosophers* in the Libreria Marciana reaffirm the important presence of Veronese in the area of Piazzetta San Marco.

Our route leads across the Grand Canal to the church of San Pantaleone: this has the *Miracle of Saint Pantaleon*, one of the artist's last works.

Nearby are the Gallerie dell'Accademia, with celebrated paintings, starting with the glorious *Feast in the House of Levi*, at the centre of the famous judicial inquiry of 1573. There are two sparkling altarpieces: the *Mystic Wedding of Saint Catherine* and a youthful *Sacra Conversazione* from the church of San Zaccaria. A precious curiosity is the *Allegory of the Battle of Lepanto*.

This tour devoted to Veronese ends at the Zattere in the church of San Sebastiano, which contains the painter's tomb. It is wholly covered

with Veronese's paintings: from the altarpiece to the frescoes in the presbytery and decorations on the ceiling.

The museum of Torcello preserves works from the church of Sant'Antonio: the *organ panels* and the *Stories of Saint Christina*.

Veneto

The churches of Veronese's birthplace contain only two paintings, but they are of the first importance: the *Marogna Altarpiece* in San Paolo and the *Martyrdom of Saint George* in San Giorgio in Braida.

The Museum of Castelvecchio, also in Verona, possesses a select group of works, notable among them the *Bevilacqua-Lazise Altarpiece*, the artist's first important painting.

In Padua, the high altars of the Cathedral of Montagnana and the basilica of Santa Giustina still have *altarpieces* by Veronese.

The sketch for the *Martyrdom of Santa Giustina* and a large *Altarpiece* from the abbey of Praglia are in the Civic Museum of Padua.

In Vicenza the basilica of Santa Corona contains a luminous *Adoration of the Magi*; the Civic Art Gallery exhibits a very fine *Madonna and Saints*, while the "Sala del Quadro" of the Santuario del Monte Berico houses the *Feast of Saint Gregory*, the only one of these banqueting scenes, one of Veronese's specialities, still in its original setting.

Florence

Florence is, after Venice, the city with the largest number of paintings by Veronese: about fifteen canvases are in the Uffizi and Pitti galleries and there are others elsewhere.

The best known are probably

the *Madonna with Saint Barbara* and the Uffizi *Annunciation*, but special mention must be made of the *Portrait of Giuseppe da Porto and His Son* in the Contini Bonacossi Collection.

Rome

Rome has twenty or so paintings, held in museums and private collections. The unusual *Saint Antony Preaching to the Fishes* in the Borghese Gallery, which also has a vigorous *John the Baptist Preaching*.

The Pinacoteca Capitolina and the Pinacoteca Vaticana possess a group of interesting youthful *Allegories*. A vast canvas with the *Marriage at Cana* is in the Palazzo di Montecitorio.

Lombardy

In the Napoleonic period a number of large canvases were taken to the Pinacoteca di Brera in Milan. They include the *Feast in the House of Simon*, the Baptism of Christ and the late, deeply moving *Christ Supported by an Angel*. Other outstanding works are in churches in the city and province of Brescia.

Other Locations in Italy

A small group of works is in Puglia; the most interesting is the *Deposition* in the church of Ostuni.

A version of the *Feast in the House of Simon* and other fine paintings are in the Galleria Sabauda, Turin. Collections in Genoa number about a dozen paintings by Veronese, including a *Judith and Holofernes* in the Museum of the Palazzo Rosso.

The *complex of organ panels* from San Geminiano are in the Galleria Estense in Modena, while in Rimini the *Martyrdom of Saint Julian* embellishes the church of the same name.

Finally, there is a large *Baptism of Christ* in the parish church of Latisana (Udine).

Works Abroad

Paolo Veronese has always been one of the most sought after artists internationally. His sumptuous compositions, profane subjects, and luminous colours have attracted collectors all over the world, and his works occupy a leading place in many private and public collections. This is shown eloquently by the large number of paintings in Vienna (about thirty) and Madrid (about ten) in museums formed from the Hapsburg collections.

Vienna

The array of paintings at Vienna's Kunsthistorisches Museum opens with works from the early period, like the virtuoso piece, *Marco Curzio*, and the Mannerist *Consecration of David*. They include an outstanding sequence of Gospel scenes painted around 1580, such as the very fine *Christ and the Woman with the Issue of Blood*. A typical example of the Hapsburg collections was the intense *Lucrece*.

Madrid

The Prado possesses some delightful canvases with mythical subjects, like *Venus and Adonis*, and some examples of sacred subjects handled as sumptuous profane scenes, such as the *Finding of Moses*. More complex are the large canvases like the youthful *Christ Among the Doctors* and virile *Christ and the Centurion*.

Paris

The Louvre contains a spectacular series of fifteen canvases by Veronese. Some, like the gigantic *Marriage at Cana* (formerly in the refectory of San Giorgio Maggiore and recently restored) and the oval with *Jove Striking Down the Vices with Thunderbolts* (formerly in the Doge's Palace) were brought to Paris as booty during the Napoleonic campaigns.

The museum also possesses one of the best-known portraits of the artist in *La Bella Nani*.

Other French museums also possess his works; noteworthy are the *Paradise* in Lille and the *Temptations of Saint Antony* in Caen.

Britain

British collectors have always been drawn to Veronese, carefully selecting the paintings they purchased. Museums in Britain and Ireland contain a number of very fine works, about a dozen in the National Gallery, London, alone: the most striking composition is the *Family of Darius Before Alexander*; there are also the four famous *Allegories of Love* and the enchanting *Dream of Saint Helena*.

Germany

The situation in Germany is similar. Here, too, paintings by Veronese are to be found in various museums, with a large nucleus in Dresden. In the Gemäldegalerie there are fifteen paintings, including four immense and splendid canvases painted in 1571 for the Cuccina family. The Stuttgart gallery has two *Scenes of the Life of Saint Christina* from the same series that is preserved at Torcello.

Among Paolo's paintings in the Alte Pinakothek in Munich is the unusual *Cupid with Two Dogs*.

St. Petersburg and Northern Europe

The presence of Paolo's works in the Hermitage at St. Petersburg is also due to aristocratic connoisseurs. They include a small *Adoration of the Magi* on copper, a delightful *Sacra Conversazione* (an early work) and the late, intense *Dead Christ*.

The Gallery of the castle of Prague has two great canvases, *Christ Washing the Feet of His Disciples* and the *Adoration of the Shepherds*, from a cycle that is divided between the world's museums.

Collections in Budapest, Stockholm and Göteborg also have works by Veronese.

United States and Canada

A further demonstration of Veronese's popularity is the number of works in North America. Over twenty cities in the US and Canada have his paintings. Noteworthy in the collection of the Metropolitan Museum, New York, are the noble *Portrait of Alessandro Vittoria* and *Mars and Venus*. Boston's Museum of Fine Arts has the small and precious painted *chair-backs*; in Ottawa there is the *Dead Christ Supported by Angels*, the upper part of a dismembered altarpiece.

1

1. Bevilacqua-Lazise Altarpiece, *1548, canvas, 223 × 182 cm. Verona, Museo di Castelvecchio.* This painting, which is in poor condition, takes its name from the family of patrons, who are portrayed in the lower part. It is Veronese's first independent work which was executed when, at the age of twenty, he had just left Antonio Badile's workshop in Verona. There are many signs that point to the fact that this is the work of a beginner. For example, direct references to contemporary Venetian painting are lacking, the figures are somewhat awkward and the structure of the composition has been simplified. On the other hand, the young artist already displayed here what were to become some of the most characteristic features of his painting, that is to say the use of light, transparent colour and an organisation of the image which makes use of a classical architectural setting.

2

3

4

2. The Temple of Fame,
1551, detached fresco,
353 × 168 cm. Castelfranco
Veneto, Cathedral.
This is the largest surviving
fragment of the fresco from the
Villa Soranzo, decorated by
Veronese and Zelotti in 1551,
and demolished after part of it
came away in 1818. In this, one
of his earliest ornamental
frescoes with an allegorical
theme, Paolo at once revealed

his fresh and imaginative
composition and virtuoso
handling of perspective.
The clear lighting and solid
reality of the figure actually
embody a cultural inspiration
drawn from Michelangelo and
Raphael.

3, 4. Justice and
Temperance, *1551, detached*
frescoes, 200 × 100 cm.
Castelfranco Veneto, Cathedral.

Also from the Villa Soranzo,
these frescoes of winged putti
and two symbolic figures of
Virtues are in the sacristy of
Castelfranco cathedral. The
allegory is animated by a full
and brilliant vitality, the
hallmark of Veronese's art. The
splendid, sturdy girls fulfil the
ideal of fair, full-bodied beauty
that, largely due to Veronese,
became typical of Venetian
painting.

5

5. The Temptation of Saint Anthony, *1552, canvas, 198 × 151 cm, Caen, Musée des Beaux-Arts.*
Commissioned by Cardinal Ercole Gonzaga, the altarpiece was executed for one of the new altars in Mantua cathedral which had been rebuilt by Giulio Romano. Here Veronese felt the strong call of Mannerist painting, especially in the muscular body of the devil. Besides, in the female figure he experimented for the first time with a characteristically
seductive image of beauty in full bloom, which was to appear many times in his painting.

6. Juno Pouring Her Gifts Upon Venice, *1553–1554, canvas, 365 × 147 cm. Venice, Doge's Palace, Sala del Consiglio dei Dieci.*
When he was only just twenty-five years old Veronese's fame had spread to all the territory of the Venetian Republic. Thus he decided to move to Venice, where he soon received praise, honours and important commissions. On
the advice of a minor painter, Giovan Battista Ponchino, the young Veronese was summoned, together with Zelotti, to decorate the ceilings of a number of chambers which were intended for the Consiglio dei Dieci, the very influential magistracy that had its seat in Doge's Palace. This luminous allegory stands out among Veronese's many paintings; indeed, it has rightly become one of the symbolic images of the splendour of Venice in the middle of the 16th century.

8

7. Giustiniani Altarpiece,
1553–1555, canvas,
313 × 190 cm. Venice,
San Francesco della Vigna.
This was the first altarpiece
Veronese painted in Venice and
it contained explicit references to
the Pesaro Altarpiece, *painted*
by Titian thirty years previously.
The figures are, in fact, disposed
in the same compositional
pattern, while the areas of
colour are applied translucently
and lightly. From this point of

view, from the 1550s onwards,
the development of Veronese took
a noticeably different direction
from that of Titian and
Tintoretto, who were seeking an
ever thicker, mellower colour.

8. The Coronation of Esther,
1556, canvas, 450 × 370 cm.
Venice, San Sebastiano.
Veronese worked on a number
of occasions in the church of
San Sebastiano, covering almost
every available space with

paintings. Among his most
spectacular works the most
notable are the three large
panels set in the wooden ceiling,
which are, therefore, to be
observed sotto in su.
The Coronation of Esther
is the central episode; the
monumental composition,
brimming over with light,
glowing colours and sumptuous
dress, is seen against a clear
blue sky, which further
embellishes the scene.

10

9. The Triumph of Mordecai, 1556, oval canvas, 500 × 370 cm. Venice, San Sebastiano.
This is another panel from the ceiling of the church. Stimulated by the setting, Veronese daringly foreshortened the scene, with great rearing steeds that seem to be rushing towards the observer. The excellent condition of the San Sebastiano paintings allows Veronese's colours to be admired in all their splendour.

10. Music, 1556-1557, circular canvas, diameter 230 cm. Venice, Libreria Marciana.
This composition is also situated on a ceiling, which therefore implies a particular type of perspective. In competition with another six painters of his own age, Veronese was the winner and obtained a prize from Titian, who awarded him a gold medal. Of the three tondi executed for the ceiling of the Libreria Marciana, Music is the most celebrated, due to the well-balanced composition and the great richness of the colour, which resembled that used thirty or forty years previously by the young Titian.

11

11. The Supper at Emmaus,
1559-1560, canvas,
290 × 448 cm. Louvre, Paris.
This very successful composition,
which was part of Cardinal
Richelieu's collection, was so
famous that it influenced

the development of French
18th-century painting. It is one
of the first examples of the
celebrated "feasts," in which
Veronese included, together with
the characters of the Gospel
story, dozens of other figures.

However, it should be noted
that Christ and the disciples of
Emmaus are in fact separated
from the other guests, who
in any case, are all bound
together by very close
compositional links.

13

Decoration of Villa Barbaro, ca. 1560, frescoes in five rooms and the central hall, Maser (Treviso).
This cycle of frescoes, executed by Veronese in the villa built by Palladio for the brothers Marcantonio and Daniele Barbaro, was one of the supreme achievements, not only of the artist himself, but also of Renaissance painting taken as a whole. Palladio's luminous architectural structure allowed Veronese to work in large spaces and in rooms disposed according to a logical pattern. The themes of the frescoes follow a complex iconographic scheme (probably specified by the Barbaro brothers, who were both committed intellectuals), but Veronese was able to transform each allegory, even the most abstruse, into figures that were tangible, credible and joyous. Overall the frescoes can be defined as a triumph of agricultural labour. But this subject (skilfully presented with a helping hand from the real landscape, visible through the large windows) was a mere pretext for Veronese. A large number of optical effects are mingled with the presence of male and female figures, which are nearly always images of blooming and totally satisfying beauty. The transparency of Veronese's colour and the brightness of his light here reach a high point, which would then be sought after by the great painters of the Venetian Settecento, in particular Sebastiano Ricci and Giambattista Tiepolo.

12. Little Girl at a Doorway.
This is perhaps the most famous detail of all the Maser frescoes. The smiling child opens a false door, painted in the central hall of the villa. The effect is one of great charm and grace.

13. Harmony.
It decorates one of the walls of the Stanza del Tribunale d'Amore, in which the frescoes allude to the virtues of married life.
Veronese was always fond of the theme of music; he never missed the opportunity to interpret it afresh. A curious detail in this room is the way Veronese has painted his own work shoes, which have been left at the base of a short wall. This would seem to suggest that the room was the last to be decorated.

14

14. Allegory of the Summer
and the Autumn.
*It is one of the large lunettes in
the Sala dell'Olimpo, in which
the triumph of the fruits of
agriculture is celebrated. The
scene is dominated by the
mythological figures of Ceres
(crowned with ears of corn) and
Bacchus (with grapes), which
symbolise the abundance of
grain and vine in the summer
and autumn.*

15

15. Girl with Her Nurse
Appearing at a Balcony.
The largest room (called Sala
dell'Olimpo) is divided half-way
up the wall by a false
balustrade. The two women are
standing opposite two young
gentlemen; the elderly nurse
points them out to the beautiful
but inattentive girl. The use
of the twisted columns is worthy
of note; this is the only slight
exception to a division of space
for which Veronese normally
used fluted, Ionic or Corinthian
columns.

16. The Marriage at Cana,
1562–1563, canvas,
669 × 990 cm.
Paris, Louvre.
This is one of the largest and
most sumptuous "feasts,"
originally in the refectory of San
Giorgio Maggiore in Venice.
Were it not for the presence,
which is clearly stressed, of
Christ and Mary at the centre of
the table, the enormous painting
might well be thought to be
totally profane and to be,
therefore, the magnificently
imaginative depiction of an
enormous wedding feast of
Veronese's day. In the group
of musicians in the centre the
portraits of Veronese, Tintoretto
and Titian have been identified,
while historical personages are
hidden among the figures, which
amount to over a hundred.

16

17

17. The Family of Darius before Alexander, *ca. 1565, canvas, 93 × 187 cm. London, National Gallery. Similar to the paintings in the presbytery of San Sebastiano as far as its compositional scheme is concerned, this work is one of Veronese's most famous, especially due to the excellent condition of the splendid colours and the sumptuousness of the dress and armour. As is often the case, sharply-drawn classical architecture appears in the background.*

19

18. Saint Anthony, Saint Cornelius and San Cipriano, *ca. 1567, canvas, 180 × 270 cm. Milan, Brera. Although he adopted a traditional triangular scheme, Veronese managed to confer an intensely lively air to the scene thanks to the delicate way he depicted the light, which seems to be warmed in the interior lined with precious marble and glittering gold.*

19. The Dream of Saint Helen, *ca. 1570, canvas, 197 × 115 cm. London, National Gallery. Only very rarely was Veronese able to concentrate on a single figure. In this case the vision of the Cross on the part of Saint Helen takes place by an open window. The handling of the paint, applied with thin glazes, makes this one of Veronese's most delicate works.*

Following pages
20. Christ and the Centurion, *1571, canvas, 192 × 297 cm. Madrid, Prado. This is the best version of a theme that was repeatedly tackled by the artist, who here managed to create an atmosphere of moving sentiment. The space between Christ and the ageing centurion on his knees becomes a deep abyss into which pain and hope descend.*

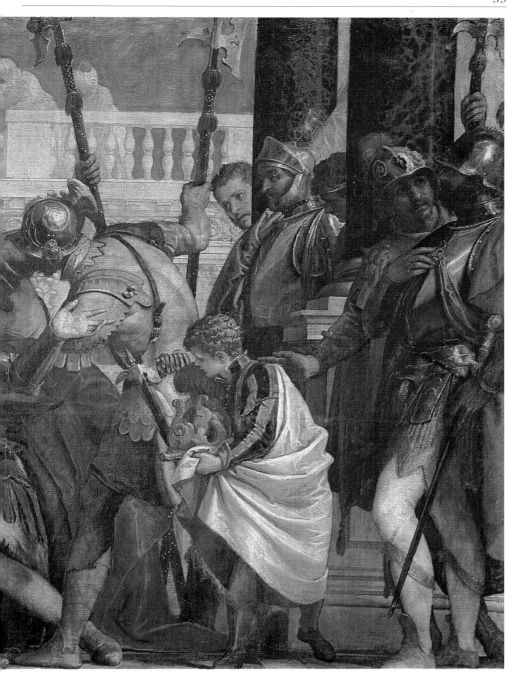

21

21. The Feast of Saint
Gregory, *1572, canvas,
477 × 862 cm. Vicenza,
Santuario di Monte Berico.*
In 1848 the painting was cut
to pieces by the bayonets of the
Austrian soldiers. The thirty-two
fragments, each of them badly
torn, were pieced together with
great patience, but here and
there areas of restoration are
noticeable.
Despite these vicissitudes, it is
still an eloquent example of
Veronese's ability to conceive
and control the treatment
of his "feasts."
The episode recounted is that
of the miraculous presence
of Christ as a pilgrim at one
of the customary suppers offered
by the saint to the poor.
Particularly effective is the
contrast between the poor clothes
of the beggars and the
sumptuous costumes of the pages
and prelates.

22

22–24. The Feast in the
House of Levi, *1573, canvas,
555 × 1280 cm. Venice,
Gallerie dell'Accademia.
Once again resplendent after
recent restoration, this is the
largest and most famous of
Veronese's "feasts," particularly
as a result of the charge of*
"indecency" *levelled against it
by the Inquisition.
Originally in the refectory of
SS. Giovanni e Paolo in Venice
(with the title of* Last Supper*),
it was subsequently slightly
retouched by the artist, who
also changed the title.
Through the great number*
*of episodes which are narrated
visually without any
interruptions, the scene develops
as a sequence of events and
personages that are, however,
all linked by the very effective
architectural setting and
the refined brilliance of
the colours.*

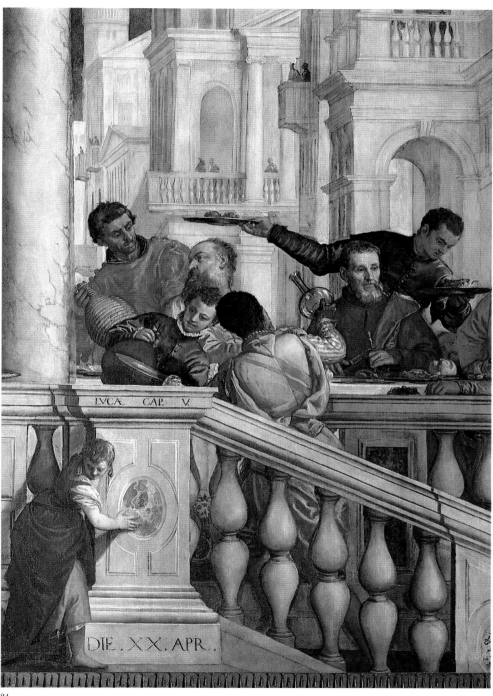

26

25. Venice Welcomes Justice and Peace, *1575–1577, canvas, 250 × 180 cm. Venice, Doge's Palace, Sala del Collegio. This is one of the principal compositions in the ceiling of the chamber, which Veronese executed with the assistance of his brother, Benedetto Caliari. Once again the ability to transform an allegorical theme into a realistic scene was added to the brilliant use of perspective.*

26. Dialectics, *1575–1577, canvas, 150 × 220 cm. Venice, Doge's Palace, Sala del Collegio. The side panels of the ceiling are painted in frames with particular shapes. This did not prevent Veronese from including delightful female figures, alluding to various virtues, in works which displayed great charm and limpid colour.*

28

27. The Mystic Marriage
of Saint Catherine, *ca. 1575,
canvas, 337 × 341 cm.
Venice, Gallerie dell'Accademia.*
*The taste for exceptionally rich
colour here reaches a degree of
magnificence which had already
been extolled by contemporary
writers: "One might say that the
Painter, for this effect / Has
mixed pearls, rubies and gold /
And the finest sapphire and
emerald / And diamonds so
pure, so perfect." / (Boschini,
1660)*

28. The Allegory of Love III
(Respect), *ca. 1570, canvas,
185 × 193 cm. London,
National Gallery.*
*This is the third episode in a
group of four allegories of love,
originally located on the ceiling
of a Venetian palace. Their
former location explains the
unusual perspective chosen
by the painter.*

30

29. Mars and Venus Bound
by Cupid, *ca. 1580, canvas,*
206 × 161 cm. New York,
Metropolitan Museum.
It is probable that this delightful
picture was painted by Veronese
for the collection of Emperor
Rudolph II, who was
particularly fond of this kind of
theme combining eroticism and
moralism. Also the execution,
with rich expanses of colour,
athletic bodies and ivory skin, is
a vivid reminder of Rudolph's
taste.

30. The Rape of Europa,
ca. 1580, canvas,
240 × 303 cm.
Venice, Doge's Palace,
Sala dell'Anticollegio.
In the past this composition
enjoyed great celebrity. The very
graceful figure of Europa seated
on a white bull, and the
melancholy atmosphere which
the marvellous colours emanate,
was to be a valuable source
of inspiration for Tiepolo.

31

31. Venus and Adonis,
ca. 1580, canvas,
212 × 191 cm.
Madrid, Prado.
This painting is an excellent
example of Veronese's poetic
interpretation of mythological
themes during his last period.

While the colours are still
very limpid, the costumes
exhilaratingly sumptuous and
the bodies extremely beautiful,
the light thickens and is no
longer perfectly translucent, but
seems almost to be veiled by the
approaching sunset.

32

32. The Agony in the
Garden, *1581, canvas,*
108 × 80 cm. Milan, Brera.
In Veronese's last years a vein
of melancholy, sometimes even
of anguish, crept in. The flashes
of light, harsh and
unpredictable, which are
reflected in this painting are a
moving demonstration of this.
The return to rhythms of a
Mannerist nature in the figures
is also interesting.

33

33. Judith and Holofernes,
1581, canvas, 195 × 176 cm.
Genoa, Galleria di Palazzo
Rosso.
*The contrast between the light
flesh tones of the fair and
graceful Judith and the dark
skin of the slave, almost causes
us to forget the terrible theme
of the beheading of Holofernes.
The dark background exalts the
brilliant colours, which include*

*principally a vivid range
of whites and reds.*

34. The Triumph of Venice,
1583, oval canvas,
904 × 580 cm. Venice,
Doge's Palace, Sala del
Maggior Consiglio.
*This was Veronese's last great
composition, set in the ceiling
of the large meeting chamber
of the Venetian patrician order.*

*Although he was helped by
assistants, once again Veronese
displayed his matchless talent for
composing scenes of rejoicing.
On the other hand it is possible
to perceive a change in the
political situation. After the war
of Cyprus with the Turks and
the plague of 1576 the Venetian
economy was under a strain
and, from a historical point of
view, there was little to celebrate.*

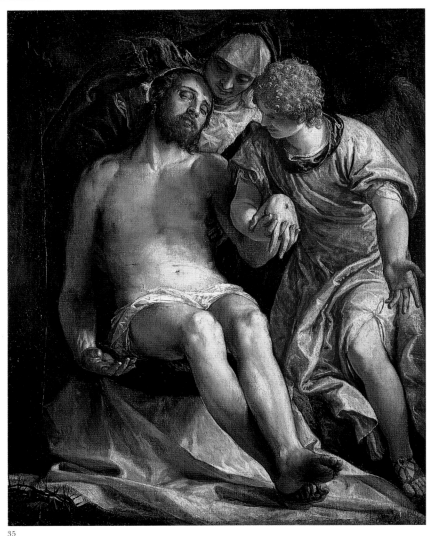

35

35. Dead Christ, the Madonna and an Angel, *ca. 1585, canvas, 147 × 111 cm. St. Petersburg, Hermitage. Veronese's life was not particularly long; the artist died in 1588 at the age of sixty. Besides, in the last years of his life he painted very little—this was probably a sign that his health was deteriorating. Perhaps for this reason his last works often reflected themes that were full of pathos. Thus the artist who, more than any other, was able to create a sort of Olympus on earth, filling his great paintings and frescoes with figures that exuded energy and vitality, concluded his career by repeatedly painting images of Christ who was suffering or dead. Of these, the St. Petersburg painting is perhaps the most noteworthy.*

Anthology of Comments

Likewise Paolo Veronese, a painter who enjoys a high reputation in Venice today, though not yet more than thirty years old, has produced many praiseworthy paintings...

In the Sala del Gran Consiglio he made a large painting [which was destroyed by fire in 1577] of Frederick Barbarossa before the Pope, with a large number of figures in different poses and garments, all of them beautiful and truly representing the court of a Pope and an emperor and the Venetian Senate, with many gentlemen and senators of that Republic portrayed from life: and, in short, for size, design and beautiful and varied attitudes, this work is rightfully praised by all.

(Giorgio Vasari, *Le vite de' più eccellenti pittori, scultori et architettori*, 1568)

The commission was to paint the work [the *Feast in the House of Levi* now in the Gallerie dell'Accademia] as I thought best. It is large and can contain numerous figures, as I thought...

I paint pictures with a concern for what seems suitable, as far as my intellect can understand it.

(From the minutes of Paolo Veronese's interrogation by the Tribunal of the Inquisition, 18 July 1573)

While Tintoretto revealed in many of his works the greatest achievement of art, with the expression of his figures in erudite forms, vivid attitudes and with great style and energy of colour, composing with highly inspired thoughts that are insuperable, Veronese also, through his majestic inventions, the loveliness of the subjects, the attractiveness of their visages, the variety of their features, the beauties and infinite attractions he introduced into his works, to which he gave such elegant symmetry (commonly called grace), can be held to have adorned painting with all majesty and ornament. So that in the midst of such doubtful and uncertain disputes, all one can say is that the one was the Castor and the other the Pollux of the heavens of painting, and that like new Atlases they supported such noble burdens, both pleasing with their paintings, delighting by their various inventions and the most skilful artifices of art.

(C. Ridolfi, *Le maraviglie dell'arte*, 1648)

Oh Paulo Veronese, oh my happiness, / I put my thoughts to rights, / hoping to acquire strength and vigour from yours, / to spend the coin of my talent... / He that wishes to see ideas, let him come here, / for he will steal your heart with his works, / so that everyone will be enchanted by them. / I must tell you that if this divine Painter / had gone begging from nature, / as do certain fools here and there, / he would never have attained such honour! / His model was his mind; / nature was his own immense knowledge; his invention, his variety / were infused in him by the Lord Almighty.

(M. Boschini, *Carta del navegar pitoresco*, 1660).

The great Paolo Veronese ought to be called the

58

treasurer of painting: since it entrusted him with all the gems in its precious exchequer, with the faculty to distribute them as he willed; with the result that the whole world was bedecked with jewels by his paintbrush.
(M. Boschini, *Le ricche miniere della pittura veneziana*, 1674)

Among the most outstanding gifts which the heavens showered on him, one was his great facility and felicitousness in invention and in colouring, such that endless works came from his hand and, what is even more unusual, without the greatness of the number of them in any way taking from the perfection of each.
(F. Baldinucci, *Notizie de' professori del disegno*, 1688)

Paolo Veronese was the creator of a new manner, which soon attracted everyone's eyes. Incorrect in drawing, and even more in costumes, he revealed an indescribable facility in painting, and a touch that is enchanting. All that was beautiful or bizarre that he conceived in his imagination he would bring into his compositions to adorn them; and he omitted nothing that might make them extraordinary, magnificent, noble, rich, and worthy of great lords and princes, for whom alone he seemed to use his brush.
One is not content merely with gazing at these paintings, always embellished with beautiful and splendid buildings; one longs, so to speak, to be inside them, to walk in them as one pleases, to seek out every smallest corner. Everything in Paolo's works is

like a magic spell; and of him one can truly say that even his faults are pleasing.
(F. Algarotti, *Saggio sopra la pittura*, 1762)

One cannot seek great elegance in the nude figures in Paolo's works. His art is very distinguished in the garments, with beautiful folds of drapery, rich and majestic, in which the figures are shown in delightful poses. Paolo painted with beautiful colours, fresh, lucid and rich, and he understood well the colouring of shadows and reflections, making them as lovely as clear colours. This arose naturally out of the rapidity with which he worked, so that the colours remained pure and clear.
(A.M. Zanetti, *Della pittura veneziana*, 1771)

His talent was naturally noble, elevated, magnificent, delightful, vast; and no city of the provinces could have supplied him with ideas proportioned to that genius save Venice. [The *Triumph of Venice* in the Doge's Palace is] a compendium of these marvels with which Paolo charms the eye by presenting it with an enchanting whole which comprises parts that are all lovely: bright airy spaces, splendid buildings that almost tempt one to walk in them, joyful and elevated faces, chosen in most cases from nature and embellished by art; graceful, expressive movements, skilfully balanced against each other; garments fine in cut and drapery, crowns, sceptres and riches worthy of such august images; perspective that makes the objects seem fur-

ther away, without their looking unpleasant when seen close-up; vivid colours, either matched or contrasting, and brought together harmoniously with an art that is his alone and could not be imagined; handling of the brush that unites great speed with great intelligence, which with every touch creates, completes, and teaches—all gifts that had by that time become second nature to him, and that form the nature of his genius.
(L. Lanzi, *Storia pittorica dell'Italia*, 1795–1796)

Saint John in the Desert [no. 23 in the Galleria Doria Pamphili in Rome] by Paolo Veronese, not entirely finished, is surprising by the glowing light that surrounds all the objects. This quality is found in all the works of Veronese. How did he achieve it?
It is said that he sketched out his paintings in water colour, but this has not been proven... In general the flesh tints in Paolo Veronese's colours were sketched in with a colder tone than they were to have when they were finished. The light colours were whiter and well mixed. He returned to this sketch with *transparent colours*, and the luminous ground showed through, and this is the reason why these paintings, though vigorous, have this admirable clarity... Observations made for twenty years have led me to the conviction that fine colouring cannot be achieved save through the methods that the Venetian and Dutch painters used. I would not swear that all possessed the same method of sketching in, but all of them had the same constancy

in using transparent colours to put the final touches to their work.
(A. Costantin and Stendhal, *Idées Italiennes sur quelques tableaux célèbres*, 1831)

There is a man who is able to paint brightness without violent contrasts, who paints the *plein-air*, which we have always been told is impossibile: this man is Paolo Caliari.

To my judgement, he is perhaps the only artist that has shown himself able to grasp the secret of nature. Without needing to imitate his manner exactly, one can travel along many roads where he has placed his guiding lamps... I owe everything to Paolo Veronese.
(E. Delacroix, *Journal*, 1854)

But although thought and feeling may be slow in invading a town, fashion comes there quickly.

Spanish fashions in dress as well as Spanish ceremonial and manners, reached Verona soon enough, and in Paolo Caliari we find all these fashions reflected, but health, simplicity, and unconsciousness too.

This combination of seemingly opposite qualities forms his great charm for us today, and it must have proved as great an attraction to many of the Venetians of his own time; for they were already far enough removed from simplicity to appreciate to the full his singularly happy combination of ceremony and splendour, with an almost childlike naturalness of feeling.
(B. Berenson, *The Italian Painters of the Renaissance*, 1894)

Goodness, grace, smiling faces, opulence, nobility, prosperity, beauty, festivities, music, the countryside; flowers—and fruits; luminous, ivory, female nudes; rich stuffs—these are the outward signs of Veronese's Olympian world, lyrical with colour.

His muse knows nothing of the speculative meditation of Leonardo, nor the terror of the titanic Michelangelo, nor the torments of incessant action of Tintoretto: to all of these Paolo opposes the serenity of his inner peace, barely touched by a veil of sweet melancholy. In the dramatic period towards the end of the 16th century, he seems to have responded to the moral murkiness of the religious struggles like Epicurus, that truth lies in the certainty of sensation, the absence of pain and in tranquillity. And he banished from himself and his creations pain, evil, ugliness, death; leaving his creations to live in the eternity of his colour, like gods free from need and care in complete happiness.
(G. Delogu, *Antologia della pittura italiana*, 1939)

Veronese designed his paintings along the lines of a Mannerist drawing, and this tends to refute the common assertion that drawings are always a sign of an early creative impulse. In fact his drawings are not very unlike those of Tintoretto, and recall the Mannerist sculptors of the period. Then as he painted he seems to have cancelled or ignored them, until the twisted forms and contortions are flattened out, set naturally within the endlessly shimmering scales of colour. And while in the drawings he was

thinking of Vittoria or Campagna, by the end of the painting he was thinking of himself as Carpaccio reborn, the friend of Sanmicheli and Palladio instead of Coducci and Lombardo; or he thought of the ingenuous happiness of a youth growing up at the time of the young Titian's *Feast of Cupids*. In fact I'd say that it is Titian's antique Greek manner, the touch of Phidias about him, that is revived in Veronese and felicitously smooths out all the contrived passages of the new age. What other reason is there for one's renewed amazement on seeing how the most *recherché* and contorted gestures are wrought into the harmony of tone and attain to an Olympian calm like that of Greek pediments, seen from an unprecedented point in space?... To Veronese the world thronging before his eyes flattened like a light sumptuous tapestry that a breath of wind lifts gently from the wall, making the colours shimmer all at once. And with a gaze like his it must have been difficult to have eyes for anything save triumphs and apotheoses.
(R. Longhi, *Viatico per cinque secoli di pittura veneziana*, 1946)

How can we explain the relative lack of interest in Paolo Veronese today? To tell the truth, if it were not for Maser, he would be almost forgotten, save, of course, by art historians, who include him in their books, where a taste for beauty rarely appears. The reason may be that today's painters find nothing in his technique that can be of use to them in solving their own specific problems; and painters, as is well known, are

usually indifferent to paintings that cannot help them, in this way. Today, far more than in the past, painters guide public opinion in art matters, and Veronese cannot compete with Velázquez in technique nor with Piero della Francesca in the care taken to define the relationship between the figure and the space it is set in. Though he is equally existential and ineloquent, he appears to critics today as less severe than the Spaniard and less solemn than the Tuscan. But I disagree with this attitude. When I study the paintings of Veronese I feel such complete and perfect fulfilment that it moves my whole being, my feelings, sentiments and intellect.
(B. Berenson, in *Palladio, Veronese e Vittoria a Maser*, 1960)

Veronese's formation was influenced decisively by Mannerism, which Giulio Romano and Parmigianino spread throughout northern Italy, including the fascination of the Michelangelesque (brought to the Veneto by Ponchino); but it is also clear that subsequently his art relinquished the Mannerist tension characteristic of his contemporary Tintoretto. It seems as if the emotive force of colour redeems the abstract and tormented composition of Mannerist aesthetics. Not that Veronese entirely disowned his basic training, but he continued to make use of it in formal terms, as the framework for his imaginative colouring. As he developed, he seems to have enlivened the terms of his original poetic, subordinating every formal element to his luminous colouring: from his lu-

minous "afternoon" light (as Baudelaire termed it) he moved on to a more pathetic, crepuscular and nocturnal light that enabled him to define space in terms of light much more precisely. In this sense Veronese's art is the last great voice of the Italian Renaissance.
(R. Pallucchini, "Paolo Veronese," in *Enciclopedia Universale dell'Arte*, XIV, 1966)

The painting in Santa Corona [the *Adoration of the Magi*], at first neglected by the critics, produced an effect on me that nowadays would be described as that of a drug (the only effect, in my opinion, which one should desire of art), which is typical of Veronese's effect on the beholder. That sky and those clouds tinged with night already, yet bright, illuminated by a special kind of light-shadow or light-darkness, different from daylight yet still bright; and that sumptuous display of satins and shimmering velvets, with highly inventive perspectives that give a new meaning to the word "marvellous"—they all compose a vision of something that has never been seen, yet does not conflict with the truth, and possesses the virtue of drawing us into itself without giving us the least impression of changing our lives. In fact we delight in it, with our minds and bodies unchanged.
(G. Piovene, "Un mondo mentale," in *L'Opera completa di Veronese*, 1968)

In his vast output there are only relatively few works that are dated or can be dated by using reliable documents, and so it is hard to establish a

chronology. Besides, it has to be said that as he grew older, he did not develop a uniform style but varied it, depending on whether a painting was intended to decorate walls or ceilings and its position in relation to the eye of the viewer. Now that many paintings have been moved from their original settings, the distinction is much less clear. But with this borne in mind, it can be said that Veronese's style had a fairly limited development.
(C. Gould, "Paolo Caliari," in *Dizionario Biografico degli Italiani*, XVI, 1973)

In the midst of the oscillations of his youthful genius, there appears a progressively unifying factor in his unprecedented use of colour, still somewhat transparent, veiled with pearly grey shadows, with unusual effects of juxtaposition and contrast between warm and cold tones amid the interplay of coloured shadows. These features were very different from the "naturalism" that dominated with Titian in the Venetian art world. Instead Paolo accepted the abstract cerebralism of Mannerism. For these reasons, I feel that his work in the Libreria Marciana and, above all, on the ceiling of San Sebastiano took on a truly revolutionary character with the frescoes and canvases painted between 1556 and 1558. His youthful style here found its full maturity in the highly original interpretation of Mannerism. His aim was clearly no longer the dramatic or idyllic representation of nature, as in Titian or Bassano, nor the hallucinatory transfigurations of Tintoretto, and least of all ab-

stract subjection to the Tuscans' cult of design. Instead it was a kind of abstract and joyous contemplation of beauty, with particular affinities with the anomalous classicism of Palladio. At San Sebastiano, the individual juxtapositions of hues, the transparency of the coloured shadows, the imaginative and imposing world of the composition, all create an unforgettable impression of a luminous, Olympian and festive sense of beauty.
(T. Pignatti, "Paolo Veronese," in *Da Tiziano a El Greco. Per la storia del Manierismo a Venezia*, 1981)

Veronese, too, fled into an exile far more ideal and Edenic than Palladio's, a flight made possible by the exceptional nature of the Venetian Republic. The real alternative of numerous Venetian nobles was to increase the Italian colony in Calvinist Geneva or follow Marcantonio Thiene's diplomatic exile to the court of France. Veronese remained faithful to the cultural unity of the Renaissance, naturally translated into the abstract schemes of the aristocratic society he belonged to and identified himself with... His art is wholly profane in the sense that it is wholly sacred; in his paintings Christ (as in the Gospel) mixes with Magdalenes and mercenaries, in the most picturesque places, where there may even be one figure set apart and wiping the blood flowing from his nose.
(S. Marinelli, "Premessa a Veronese," in *Veronese a Verona*, exhibition catalogue, 1988)

In the last years of Veronese's life, there emerged a new expressive fervour of unprecedented profundity. The source of it was perhaps the anguish caused by too many commitments, his ill health, and a new cultural tendency, or possibly a combination of all these elements and yet others that we can only imagine. Be that as it may, it was not a sudden change but one that emerged slowly, like a new language to be used only if necessary... Even the subjects in which such deep feeling was not necessary were charged with visionary intensity.
(W. R. Rearick, "Paolo Veronese. La vita e l'opera," in *Paolo Veronese. Disegni e dipinti*, exhibition catalogue, 1988)

Essential Bibliography

Palladio, Veronese e Vittoria a Maser, Milan 1960.

L. Crosato, *Gli affreschi delle Ville Venete*, Milan 1962.

F. Zava Boccazzi, *Veronese*, Milan 1964.

T. Pignatti, *Paolo Veronese a Maser*, Milan-Geneva 1965.

T. Pignatti, *Le pitture di Paolo Veronese nella chiesa di San Sebastiano*, Milan 1966.

R. Marini, *L'opera completa del Veronese*, Milan 1968.

R. Marini, *Tutta la pittura di Paolo Veronese*, Milan 1968.

Cinquant'anni di pittura veronese, exhibition catalogue, Museo di Castelvecchio, Verona 1974.

T. Pignatti, *Veronese*, Venice 1976, new edition 1993.

P. Ticozzi, *Paolo Veronese e i suoi incisori*, Milan 1976.

P. Ticozzi, *Immagini dal Veronese*, Rome 1978–79.

Da Tiziano a El Greco. Per la storia del Manierismo a Venezia, exhibition catalogue, Doge's Palace, Venice 1981.

D. Rosand, *Painting in Cinquecento Venice: Titian, Veronese, Tintoretto*, New Haven-London 1982.

Splendours of Venice. 1500–1600, exhibition catalogue, Royal Academy of Art, London 1983.

R. Pallucchini, *Veronese*, Milan 1984.

R. Cocke, *Veronese's Drawings. A Catalogue Raisonné*, London 1986.

Paolo Veronese. Disegni e dipinti, exhibition catalogue, Fondazione Cini, Venice 1988.

Veronese e Verona, exhibition catalogue, Museo di Castelvecchio, Verona 1988.

Le siècle de Titien, Giorgione, Veronese, exhibition catalogue, Paris 1993.